OPHELIA
RISING

O.R.

Punk ★ Hostage ★ Press

Ophelia Rising
Copyright © O.R. 2023
ISBN: 978-1-940213-25-5
An Imprint of Punk Hostage Press

EDITED BY
Iris Berry

INTRODUCTION
A. RAZOR

FOREWORD
Nicca Ray

COVER ART
Rhea Adri

Punk ★ Hostage ★ Press
Hollywood, USA
punkhostagepress.com

To my three, my daughters

The sun, the moon and the stars.

I must have dreamt you into existence. I should have named you after constellations or the bare places on earth, untouched. My three indomitable spirits. The ropes that keep me tethered to you will bear the weight of a hundred wars. I held myself to this earth because when you called me mother I needed to be there to answer. I did not recognize myself until I held you and I was not complete until you all came into being. I give to you my words and my love.

TABLE OF CONTENTS

FOREWORD

What happens to lost daughters trying to find their way home with the only road map being the bowing palm trees pointing the path? Where does love exist if not for raw lips and feet bloodied from the chase? Falling for men whose kisses promise life but whose legs disappear when the time comes to rest in the arms of permanence. What happens to the girl who loses herself? In OPHELIA RISING we follow her through abandon, witness her rising and experience her transcendence. A feat not for the squeamish these poems bring us up close and inside the internal world of a girl discovering the self she lost along the way. "I would want to be who I was in the beginning/But the world hid her from me, O.R. writes. The heroine in these exquisitely written poems runs through the arms of strangers looking for the nurture she never got. There is a sense throughout that there was never a mother for her to run to; that her mother was also a lost daughter, running. In a later poem O.R. tells whoever sees her mother to tell her she has "suffered her fate but has triumphed in her wake." And she has. In becoming a woman she has become a mother and in motherhood comes into being.

Nicca Ray, author of *Ray by Ray*

INTRODUCTION

Sometimes you will find great poets when you look hard enough for them, and sometimes great poets will find you when you least expect it. This poet found me and they really impressed me with their lines, worked out of vivid emotional states that exist paradoxically in simultaneous threads of creation and destruction. Descriptions of breaking apart on the inside of ourselves and what that can create amidst the chaos of our common withdrawal as we turn inward into unknown depths, while outwardly seeming to only be able to go thru motions, keep up appearances, show up for our everyday lives and still live them even though our internal selves are fractured, pieces missing, barely holding what's left together.

Poems like these speak of survival in a submergence of disem-powerment and turn toward a hopeful light of power not able to be seen at first in the reckoning of the darkness in the deep valley of trauma many human paths of living can lead to. They can have a familiarity for those of us who have lost our way or lost our shelter or lost our love or lost ourselves. They can speak of the hard edges around co-occurring mental health crisis, broken hearted numbness that leads to disconnect and finally regaining itself, reconnection on life's terms, and every emotion that intertwines with the self-evaluation necessary to reconnoiter healing.

These lines are important and relative, they speak a truth to the power dynamic of relationships and the uneasy turmoil as the power shifts out of sync and out of control. They speak to the lost drift after trauma from abuse, the absolute of feeling diminished to less than, but finding a way back to an abundance of love in the bonds of motherhood, of parenting and feel the life force that flows between mother and child. They reveal in that relationship the most powerful and sacred human bond possible and the frailty of the world that it exists in.

These poems are worksheets about navigating loss and overcoming pain and celebrating survival as that is a spark that creates space which hopeful to one day bloom.

But, as I have said, this poet found me, I did not find them. They found me like a lost child finds a parent that has been missing them for a lifetime and had no idea how that child was or how life had turned out for them. This poet found me not as a poet, but as a child, now grown, who I had thought I might never see again after so many agonizing years apart, and behold, this child is a poet that found me.

A. Razor
Poet, Found Father

ACKNOWLEDGMENTS

I am indebted to the people who began this process with me and treated it with the utmost care and consideration. Iris and Razor, I am grateful that you saw beauty in my words and led me through the delicate placement of my work from journal entry to print. Razor & Monika thank you for the support and encouragement you so openly offer and for giving me the gift of Eva on this earth.

To my daughters, without your existence I would not be. Thank you for allowing me to grow beside you as a mother and for recognizing the humanity within me. I learned to love myself by loving you. You are beautiful and gracious beings. I hope you continue to share your gifts and your truth with this world.

My husband, a second chance, came back to me. If I believed in fate, I would believe she brought you to me when I was trying to prove her wrong. I may have always searched for your familiar smile in the faces of strangers and then when I saw it 19 years later my soul said, "where have you been, old friend". Words of healing came after your arrival and my heart began to rest in you. I cherish you and our life together.

To my parents, the beautiful people that raised me in love and warmth. May you find yourself in the lines of my poetry where I felt the most loved. Know that I believed that the baby in the basket was always meant for your doorstep and that I am proud to call myself your daughter.

For my trees, those of you who stood tall above me and allowed me to rest in your presence without fear. Thank you for allowing me to speak my truth out loud and for loving me despite it. I will always remember the hands that reached down to lift me, that found me in the darkest corners and that stayed with me while I fought through the nights, I thought I would not see the sun. You are the light, and I could not have taken the first steps to healing without you.

I – OPHELIA'S LAST WORDS

I will always be envious

of that one last breath

The world asked for thinkers

For lovers and poets

So we gave birth to our inner voices

The hushed notions of unbecoming

With each page our heavy shoulders rise

Foreign gospel grazing our skin

The softened knives we yielded with pen

These words carry the weighted soul

Unburden yourself on parchment

But we were not the cure they sought

The art survived only the page

With ink smeared cheeks

Pressed against beaten earth

They buried us with our truth

I wrote

Because I was tired

Of bleeding

Of burning at the stake

For silence

When I die

Let me remember her dancing

Just like this

Tonight

Feet barely grazing the earth

Soul reaching through the crowd

I pray she never finds her way to the water

That she burns through this life

Until there is nothing left

Just a seared path

She was here

And for a short time

I held the fire

These unreasonable hours are made for poetry

Where my fingers glide passionately over keys

My pen seeks solace from the page

Every verse escaping its place in my mind

Fatigue has released my concealed sentiments

These words forcing their existence

Birthing themselves into the cosmos

The ink will not fail to speak of our complexities

Hush mind,

this witching hour is where my demons play best with me

There was a distinct scent of magnolias

White flowers stuck to the wet pavement

And I thought it a good day to bury us

The sky would grieve this day with me

We outgrew this place

Like the overflowing potholes

Dirty streets that left smudges on our faces

The orange groves won't hide your sin for long

Life in a citrus fog, it's clear now

What must be done

Submerge the naiveties of our youth

We all died young

on Arlington Avenue

Under the pressure of unworthy hands

These precious things will break

You are art

A mosaic of memory

Crushed glass on canvas

Brush strokes reveling in your graceless figure

Your imperfections formidable against the flawless back light

You are my art

Photographs penetrating through me

Developing a permanence in my being

If these walls could project our love

Then you would solely know my heart

I send you these lovers kisses

The ones I have no right to give

Clinging to your midnight whispers

Holding fast, though chance be dim

These hours lost to costly choices

What we break, be sure to mend

In silence unforgiving voices

Sentencing my heart to him

This world was never meant to fit the expanse of your wings

Nor accommodate your flight

You will always strain against their steel cages

Forbidden love written into your palms

The universe expands to meet the depths of your eyes

With dreams too big for the small towns in which you hide

You love too much and too soon

They will build monuments to honor you in death

But will they throw stones while you still breathe

We live on borrowed time

A path we cannot choose

Play your efforts against mine

But I refuse to lose

The song stays on repeat

It sings eternally

To tell me love be blind

But ours is deaf and mute

Writer's block

A prolonged pause of mind

I do not know if I can bleed out anymore of you

Onto these lifeless pages

Until nothing of myself remains

Put pressure on these pulsing words

I refuse to let goodbye slip past my pen

You will be my unfinished stanza

A lament to a barren love

There will be no end to us

My open book

My love

I lose myself when I become the poet

I could see the question

Shaping itself from his rearview mirror

My glassy eyes fixated on a place or a time

I would not let him follow

Walls of blue glass reflecting light on the passing traffic

White coats floating through sliding doorways

Was I locked in or were you locked out

Had freedom always tasted like the inside of my cheek

My mind becomes a dance of static emotion

Trying to solve world hunger and my own bulimia

If I could just make the puzzle fit back together

Before the missing pieces and bent edges

I return my focus to the conversation

in a maze of disorienting sentiments

Do you miss it?

No

But I do miss being understood by the people inside those walls

I shut my eyes and open them until the road ahead reappears

The world becomes too big again

I sought you out at winter's door

Succumbing to translucent storms

Clouds bereft with springs ascension

Shared visions draped in green

The waters clear away the sweet smell of you

Memories soaked in summer fleeting

Lay low my beggars' heart, this pleading soul

Still thrives my love for you

A sky glossed over in bittersweet laments

A swelling bed of lilac hues

Here I wait for your return

Love her softly

Never disturb her guarded walls

Be the voice she hears above the rest

Whispering her worth

While others rip at her seams

Love her gently and leave no damage

The mountains you must move of her insecurities

The worlds you will conquer for her to wander

From grace I've fallen for you

In our final moments I understood

hate had a stronger god

And love was a beaten heap in a corner

Shallow eyes that still showed signs of light

I screamed at her to play dead

She would not let me save her

I stayed by her side, until you stopped

Loves last stand, crippled and cowering

Pride delivers the last blow, while ego waits patiently

to feed on the remains of us

We die clinging to the beautiful lie that love conquers all

I won't touch you

Your skin is opium to my pain

I stare much too long

Lingering on the distance

Questioning your intentions

Embracing would cost me my sanity

I am gripping it like shards of glass

Squeezing the edges

Reminding me that this one will cut deeper

There is no tourniquet, no cure

A quiet pulse, like rain pattering on a car window

Lulling me to sleep in a back seat

Exchanging kisses to ease painful realities

Love me one second longer

And I will live for that

When I miss you

I write you into my stories, my poetry

You will live eternally in my words

A reminder that some love

Cannot exist beyond the page

We were born from summer storms

Autumn could not hold us

But winter calls you back to me

Yet spring will never know us

From here I can see the sun setting

Over a cookie cut rooftop

Houses that shrink the sky into small portraits

Placed delicately on window sills

The pink and orange tint of heaven fading

Already falling upon the tops of fence posts

I am left with dirty grey hues and tarnished efforts

Feet perched lightly on a ledge

Resting the weight of tomorrow on weary hands

Elbows tightly tucked into a shrinking frame

Night after night, we wait

With each closing day

We find ourselves again

In the space between

I did not need to hear the goodbyes

from your lips

I felt each one of them

When we kissed

I let you go

My poetry has mercy

And keeps you alive

I long for my solitude

It is where I dwell with common souls

They tolerate me in their shadows

And speak to my silence

Dearest self

Today I require my solitude from you

The sound of clinking ice in a glass

The soothing scent of wild lavender

Caressing the senses back from the depths

A book that gives what life denies

And a soft place to lay my head

I'll return shortly to the tight chest of yesterday

The constant gnawing of nails and skin

Today please let me be

We have loved in a thousand lifetimes

And in each one

you have coursed through my being

with hazy intent

Leaving my lips raw and feet bloodied from the chase

Born again into a tragedy of bemused fate

Sand trapped in a glass, hours squandered to foolish youth

My lifespan is shortening as are my breaths

These feeble legs can run no more

Slow your pace my love

Ease my burning lungs

And walk with me at last

Stay with me

Until always ends

His lips may be the only cure

They drip of novocain

The only touch her skin allows

To ease her tender pain

Numb away the other's marks

And clear away their stain

One kiss to heal her past assaults

Leave her better than she came

I am well versed in everything love is

Only by grasping quickly all that it is not

You don't have to speak to me in whimsical notions

I already know your heart

She will be your Saturday

Wild, free and young

I will stay your Sunday love

My arms will be your home

Her greatest gift was unconditional love

The double edge of her misfortunate end

I will compose for you a love story

Tangled limbs altering my poetry

Unraveling words in arrant symmetry

Devotion thickening in each line

Succumbing to this nameless state

We lay in beds of borrowed time

And when I come to write our end

I leave my heart and drop my pen

To leave it bleeding on the page

It holds our place

We cannot stay

Unwritten are the unknown words

Choking on reality until it burns

Blank spaces that will change our course

No end

Just in between

He will always be he

She will eternally be her

And that is infinitely enough

When our intent was only to love

How can we call it failure

They were but children playing with the word love

His intentions for a night not a lifetime

Summer stars churning juvenile emotions

Giants trampling daisies in dark corners

Carving out your path through her bones

You witnessed her wilting in his shade

The sun had not reached her face in years

Under this thick blanket of clouds

she had become something she had not intended

A flower picked for its beauty in its prime

Her petals falling to the earth

Rubbing dirt in old wounds

The breeze could only take them so far

She would never travel beyond the walls of her own imagination

To all the places she had longed to be

Losing herself piece by piece

Watch as young love grows old

The sun bedded itself into a pink abyss of sheeted nirvana

The seconds lay heavy, time slowed

She looked up at me,

questions behind stray hairs covering her vision

Her eyes fixated on another world

that ran on beyond a set of glass doors

The hours halting for a moment's gaze

The horizon taking its last bow to share the stage with the stars

I knew the answers her mind sought

She had become my vast and endless sky

Every particle in her body expanding

to create a universe where we can exist together

It was a pretend love story

But it was mine to tell

And I would choose my madness

over reality

For you to believe

I watched his hands play Chopin on the steering wheel

Or maybe it was Bach

Gentle taps in foreign tune

But my heart was learning the rhythm of him

The ransoms I have paid for these brief stalls in time

In and out of consciousness

Weary love, despairing in the unraveling of self

What have I become in the darkest hours

I am glad he cannot see my former likeness

In the rearview mirror

She closes in on me

Are you a writer

Was this the question

Do you commit your afflictions to the parchment

Dip your bloodied truth in ink

Are your fingers stained with loves misfortune

Smudging words on dampened cheeks

Blurred lines lingering amidst false intention

Unadulterated scripting

Subdued release

Tell me that the morning comes

The light returns to the sky

Give me empty promises of endless horizons

And I will continue

One foot, then the other

Moving forward into this endless night

Feeding my fears, leaving bread crumbs

Under the bed to fill their appetite

I will hold on to the memories

you sell for moonbeams and pennies

Emptying my pockets for dreams I cannot afford

Starving hands clinging to your spare affections

Hush now voices, I want to hear our story again

But this time leave out our beginning

I need to know that you exist in the last lines

I will save a seat for you here in between

We can change in the space of now and then

I wonder what it will feel like to leave this place

And breathe the air of after and unseen

Find her dancing in the rain

Bare feet at winter's door

Wrapped in blankets mid-July

Head pressed to tile floors

Hair perfect in imperfect nest

White dress with muddied hands

Not built to withstand the bending road

Or yield to life's demands

The twists of fate have curved her spine

And straightened her defense

Touched by hands that weren't as kind

She seeks one to make amends

Walk me home the long way

Running my fingers over the edges of repentance

Brushing shoulders in the vines

The air, a thick perfume

Of orange blossoms

Our children will smell of citrus and lost time

The rows of bowing palm trees

They always point towards home

Though the years have been deceiving

You are all my senses know

I refuse to leave this place

The spaces I found you in between

This is where I wait

Where time finds only a moment

To recognize us in the fleeting sunlight

Of a car sunroof

The feeling that all things last forever

We will never die here

I won't let us

There is nothing lost

To the passing of hours

Waiting

Not a second wasted on our despair

You had to learn that love

Was not pleading & longing

All so that you would recognize

His face

The moment he walked in

Dressed in all that love was

She would always be ink stained fingers and distant gaze

Unanswered prayer

The hem of a dress

Dipped in mud

Barefoot & wasted potential

There is so much

That should have been

How did you end up here

I was afraid to move

Fear of shattering floors

Delicate world beneath my feet

Breaking minds, feeble grip

Help is coming

We all wait

In silence

Alone

I was not brave

I just wanted them to know I was here

Still breathing

If found please find me

A collection of limb

& song lyrics

Light as a feather, brick heavy around neck

Last words

I will be your last victim

Severed life

I stand complete before you

I am your creation

Half sacrifice

& half art

I strung my words on tree lines

They reflected in the dawn's likeness

Stretching prose from limb to limb

I was mine and you were him

Our red and orange stained sky

Left blotted with my pen

These branches share a burden

Heavy are the thoughts of man

Reaching up to vacant skyline

Breaking boughs and battle hymn

These leaves, they fall in pages

My only hope, that you would see

But your eyes remained in places

That my soul would never be

Oh, dear girl

The skin you must shed

For them to love you

Will leave you raw & bloodied bone

You must learn to live without them

A love that's all your own

I beg you

Remember the hours with softened edge

The witty tongue that lacks the sharpened knife

Let me cradle you with affections

And stop the bleeding by my own hand

I was never well acquainted with the saints

But the angels never lost sight of me

Red hands, no fault

My beautiful Mazy

I don't think I can see a tomorrow

where I won't need your words

your laughter

I will find you in the trees and all the places

You let your love extend

Beyond your pained walls

Like reaching arms

Free from the binding earth

I will abandon my insecurities to the sky

As you would have it

Just to see your eyes in the infinite blue

You were right

I cannot see myself

As you do

I am neither brave nor strong

And in my own fight

I struggled to see yours

In the darkness

In our separate corners

The war within

Leaving us

Without you

Now we adjust our eyes to a place you

No longer dwell

I will search for you

Endlessly

In the light

II - UNBECOMING

Yes, I saw it coming

And I would choose it all again

The beginning to my end

Lost in battle

A cease fire

A break in the storm

You walked in umbrella or shield

Sheltered by your affection

I found refuge in your familiar touch

Vulnerable for the last time

I hid my sins in your light

Asking nothing of your darkness

Your kiss promised life

Read me my last rights

You know

I won't survive you

If my mind could write you the perfect song

With paper words

That I could burn to keep you warm

Would you play it on my grave

When are you done loving me

Rooms with fresh white paint

Walls with no edges

Dull razors and knives

All one-story ledges

Tranquility by the cup full

Your last stand is the blue pills

Drag your feet down vacant corridor

It's my thoughts

I'd like to kill

Not these frail bones that cheat me

Bending when I must break

Left laid to rest an empty pit

Nothing left

But my namesake

We are all open wounds to someone

You would have liked to know the girl

Before the secrets

Before the pills

I covered her mouth, a muted scream

I held her under, she looked like me

The past came digging for her bones

Her demons won

She lies alone

You would have loved the girl I was

But there is nothing left unscathed

She shined like diamonds in the dust

She poured liked Summer rain

We are those girls in bathroom stalls

Secrets etched in skin

Our stories written on the walls

Still starving from our sins

We purge our truth in porcelain sinks

And on our knees, we search for peace

Dangling limbs from boughs that break

Inhaling hell to fight our fate

We are those girls that lost our way

And those who love us

Never stayed

I pull words out of my mouth

Like mangled teeth

Pulling at the roots of self

Bleeding out my circumstance

Coughing up prose

Forcing verses out of me

These words possess me to tell my story

Impairing my sense of time

Holding me prisoner to my own mind

My message clear but goes unspoken

A silent stanza

For the broken

I can feel you leaving my system

Like alcohol running out of my veins

The taste of salt on the rim of your lips

Pouring into open wounds

The numbness settles in my finger tips

Seeing you through hazy eyes and clouded thought

Somewhere in dark alleys I still search for you

I take another drink

I emerged from the chaos of your touch

You did not witness my inept fall

I crawled into the aftermath of broken promise

Trying to find my paradise lost

Instead I awoke on deserted shores

In empty rooms with your smell

Were you stranded here once too

I can feel you down every hallway

I don't know how to leave this place

When my escape is you

I left the pages blank

Waiting for the words

They will pour out like my tears

Nothing remains with me

Trembling pen

Ink stained hands

A eulogy of lovers

You are my end

I slow the fast pace of my pulse

Easing it into the rhythm of release

I tell my reflection that this is best

The risk resonating on my shoulders

Loving you becomes a war

My mind takes shelter in deep trenches

These bullets intended for my flesh

There is no victory in your depth

I abandoned my senses

The day you smiled

My soul recognized your name

Left disarmed in a foreign place

Another casualty in your game

My heart aches

For every time I have been turned away

Love with no vacancy

Nights of endless wandering

I stand frozen at your door step

Too afraid to knock

Tell me where you tried to find her

Was she written in your veins

All I've done is try to hide her

You are digging up remains

Leave my secrets to the ground

I am buried much too deep

What is lost

I've never found

The grave is my release

Scars in the shape of handprints

Your fingertips pressed into my soul

Indentations that altered my course

I recall every memory of you

Ingesting them in these late nights

The lonely hours belonging to the ghosts of past

I cannot find my footing in this world

My mind leans on frail strangers

I listen to the rhythmic beat in empty chests

Searching for the subdued thrumming of your pulse

Finding you in everything I love

Lost in the infinite state of in between

I wait

I am writing the eulogy of us

The imagery is perfection

Dripping with the words we weep

These flowers mean to wither

Your apologies are weak

Your betrayals hidden in my script

With this longing you can keep

I want to stop writing about you

But my pen has deceived me again

Smudged in the ink ruins

Of my own undoing

Bear witness to my undoing

I disguise my naked vulnerabilities

My mysteries unraveling before you

There are wounds you cannot touch

Scars that are still painful

Be soft and I may let you read the stories

I have carved into my flesh

I can replay the memories in my head

But I cannot raise a love that did not survive

From the grave

I stand starving on the threshold

Breaking teeth on the hardened crumbs of my self-deprecation

I've sculpted piles of scavenged bones

In the likeness of what cannot be

Emptied resolve

From purging all that ached

They tore her wings out

Forbidden tongue

A girl sought after

Both pure and young

Her back hunched toward them

His intent was clear

Deep wounds part open

Beyond repair

A cruel life sentence

At the hands of men

We follow the cries of cherubic hymn

A sweet angel marred in an ungodly scene

Nothing can wash the devil's hands clean

The earth trembles to claim her as the sky turns its face

Absorbing her frailty, not a bone left in place

Take up with her in innocence

Her last fall

From grace

I divulged my shameful truth

You turned away

When you finally understood

I had done this to myself

I was both the abuser and victim

You would never forgive me

I would rather love a lie too

When she is too painful to hold

Will you still call it love

It was said you held the cure

yet you watched me choke on poison

He knew I only yearned for words

So, he held tight to the silence

She was hanging by his every word

When the noose became too tight

Fluorescent lights

One by one

Life flows in and out in passing

They pity me, their stone dispositions

Paintings in white rooms

The faces ask me, who did this to you

I cannot tell them

It was my own hand

I tighten my grip on the sheets

I hush the 10-year-old girl inside me

She points to the evasive man in a school corridor

Doors with no knobs, locks with no key

I silence the sixteen-year-old

She sways offbeat to the pills left floating in her drink

I cover the charcoal smeared lips

Of the unfamiliar woman standing before me in the mirror

I did this

But the faces already know

Wounds like this took decades to form

She lifted her open palm to the sunlight

Empty and blistered over

From holding fast to burning ropes

Knees embedded with gravel

A beggar's pose

This is what love cost me

I am more fortunate than most

And like the sun

You seared through her thinning disposition

She withered in your presence

Consuming her whole

We could not sway her to leave

Holding fast to things not meant for us

Finger tips skimming the outline

Of false hope

We kiss the flames

Embrace the embers

Tasting hell

Calling it love

Hush sweet girl

There are things you can't unsee

Softened words and affections that will never stroke your face

An altered spine leaves you open to the daggers they throw

With swift glance and sideways tongue

Your back curves in defense

You've been hit

Seek higher ground

You don't belong

You cannot dig your toes into a universe made of stone

A cage is no shelter

This foreign body

Is not your home

Tell me a story

Of who she would have been

Before the world touched her

With unworthy hands

Born of a poet

Raised by a philosopher

The only father I knew

The gifted blood

To the world I was different

To me

I was loved

He will love you

When you are soft whispers

And gentle lips

But will he love you at 3am

Thorns and offset gaze

Come back to me sweet girl

A war fought by bedside

Wild swings into dark night

We've been hit

We tell our story

The page survives us

The dry parchment soaks up our design

We meant to live fully

And die gracefully

We tell the story

Of how we wanted to be loved

In this life

And how love felt nothing as we imagined

The art and practice of living

Is to feel something

Whether it be pain

Or the tenderness love allows

We will rip ourselves in two

To prove we are not numb

We are here

It meant something

To us

I ran out of the blue pills

I do miss the silence

False prophets bottled and sold

They flatter you with stillness

Numb fingertips

A brush of melancholy

I was there inside myself

Buried alive

In the blue

There is love

& there is tragedy

You my dear are both

Look away

No sense in patching old wounds

For their comfort

I've collapsed and collected myself off bathroom floors before

Nails catch on thin skin

You waited for me to beg

Not a word, parched tongue

Muffled pleas

These muted laments

We go unseen

Wars fought inside ribcage

Mind lost outside of the body

They all look away

I would want to be who I was in the beginning

But the world hid her from me

And I don't recognize her face in the crowd

Just another nameless should have been

Slipping through the hands of strangers

I awoke to the smell of rain

And the covenant of new beginnings

Fingertips seizing the spine of deliverance

Hope fills our depths

We sacrifice self at the alter

All that has departed will return to us

A life come back to me

I looked at them in awe

I saw the fragments of myself

That I had given away

Things I lost to seconds, then decades

There in blue green eyes

All those years, safely stowed away in their tiny hands

The light had not abandoned me

It was there pulsing through them

Everything that is good would go on

Graceful beauties, gentle souls

My daughters

My immortality

I will not settle here

In this place of in between

Child huddled in a corner

An innocent casualty

Fragmented youth

Dangling suspicion

Broken bough and fragile limb

The doors never open from this side

The softest pieces of self

Frayed at the ends

I saved her for you

To love again

Don't count me out yet

I've clenched your grave markers

Between my teeth

Dirt under nails

I grew claws to get back to

Eye level with you

I knew my error, my truth

That I had taught them to bend

To cower

To apologize for existing

To beg for love

Their ears to the door

Tired eyes, swelling with their mothers'

Willingness to suffer

I cannot erase my undoing at his hands

Or what I became thereafter

There is no beauty in self destruction

No clarity within the tangled mind

I can only tell you I rose again for them

I salvaged what was left of me

To be their home

Broken windows, lost youth

Dusty corners filled with memories

The sun still shines on the weary

I am still here, my darlings

I had hoped that her end was softer

Than the knives you threw

That in the days that remained

She felt cherished

Life unfinished, faith renewed

Outside this silent prison

That she was heard, no longer mute

Holding fast to trembling frame

Falling short for sweet relief

We grasp for understanding

Through thin straws of feeble youth

Gaping mouths now frozen

She paid for lies to feel the truth

Some versus come mercifully to me in the night

Gentle hymnals, swaying soul

I set them free

Into the hollow space in between

Sonnets dampening the page

Like luke warm bath water

Passing through my hands

An exhale of smothered sorrows

Into white pillowcases

There are those pages

We do not speak of in the dark

Bared teeth grazing over sensitive skin

Splitting seams of self

I pray for deliverance

Prying open past traumas

Forcing pen to paper from the inside out

Festering prose into bitter notions

Counting the seconds to first light

Ghosts of old dancing on fragile nerves

Each word set aflame before stifled screams

Awaken you

If all I have is this savage impulse in my fingertips

Then I will write my story

Until the blood and the ink are one

I will scream out my intentions to the sleepless night

Inhaling the moons delights

Suffering at my own hand

This journey was not in vain

The words never came softly

They broke my bones & will when I birthed them into being

All I have, I have sacrificed to the pen

They won't remember me

But the art will survive us

I'd rather be buried in my truth

Then living with the stain of you

Still on my hands

I wanted to believe in good

But all I saw

Were broken women

Struggling to stand

With footprints on their back

And dirt under their nails

There was love

And there was this

The aftermath

In the dull glow

Of my own deliverance

I saw their light

Faint at first

Hands out

Reaching blindly

They rose together

One by one

Shredding the white flags of submission

Unrelenting will & force

We can no longer look away

It is time to rise with them

I am thankful for all of the pain

That had an end

For all of the hands that touched me

That can no longer cause harm

For forgiveness I was not owed but granted

And for a love I do not have to beg for

My words may not always be beautiful

The truth is a swift kick in the teeth

A hasty punch in the gut

Honesty was never well thought out

Transformation is unbecoming

I have mastered the art of suffering eloquently

Grace and steel stiffening my backbone

I was neither a rare find

Or a unique specimen

I was just another broken girl

One that needed to be walked home

And you couldn't find your legs

There are others like me

Who were forced to be a soft place for your sharp claws to stick

Women who curl their bodies inward when eyes stay lingering

On the curvature of our hips

We let distorted perceptions sit on our lap

Like suckling young

Transforming into the ghostly figures we fear most

Too familiar are the gaunt faces of our tormentors

The ungodly creatures we become crouching under the camouflage

of pulled skin and self-loathing

I look in the mirror, she is not me

I am not myself anymore

These heavy things will always be heavy

But there are moments

When another weighted soul calls you home

Sit in it with me

Lay the sadness down for just a moment

And feel the light another aching body has for you

There are sunsets

I can't replace

The soft rustling of small feet

Slowing their pace before clinging to my legs

Distant recollections

Wrapped around my fingers

I let the flood rise up and come to me

Rolling from my lips like butter

Deliverance was sifting through the muddied waters of mind

Flightless afterthoughts and shifting blame

I was not a butterfly

Transforming from one reality to the next

I was some kind of malformed entity

Sharpened with time and bitter ideals

Nerves ripened and plucked

Tensions humming under the pressure of blistered skin

The practice of stillness in shaky hands

The mimicked calm behind a gaze

This is who I am

I don't apologize for it anymore

Arms splayed out in abandon

The shame of naked wombs

Strings attached to static memories

We mourn the passing of our youth

There is no end to the unraveling

Fraying dispositions come to light

Succumbing to blind realities

The strands of fragile mind

Tiptoeing on white fences

As we straddle blades of truth

Give order to the senseless

Lost labors, empty rooms

Tell me the truth

Hope comes at a great cost

There is no cure

I have half lived as an apparition

in a bottled haze

Out of body, out of mind

Tell them

That delirium is sold on the street corners

of skid row and good intention

Victory tastes of rusted metal

Gums grinding on the prize

Their makeshift crown does not frame

the face of bastard daughters

And everything we fought to carry with us

Becomes indifference in time

We stayed much too long

Lingering on the mossy field

Coveting the possibility

Of second chance

Prolonging the Fall

Through naïve hands

Days of glory swiftly stolen

Time,

the thief of innocence

I became an afterthought

A painful recollection

Of everything you lost

They playfully pardoned us

For childish sins

Young love

Evading our inevitable

End

III - RISING

I chased the light
I became one with the sun
And when they touched me
I made them burn for it

I never knew her

I don't know if her skin felt delicate like a thin silk dress

Smooth like pressed linen

Her scent, did the air smell of lavender & loss

When she left a room

I would rather imagine what she may have been

Before me

Am I only the mirror image of her faults

Could she see all that was forbidden in my eyes

Because they were his

I know the night touched her face more often than the sun

I am a mosaic of her darkest secrets

The music called her home, I feel it

I doubt she found a love to equal her own

If there was an ending, I pray it was kinder than my beginnings

I hope she landed in a place that recognized

She was all of what might have been and nothing of what was left

In her was more sacrifice than fault

I want her to know

That I made it down the river into my mother's arms

That I became more of light than darkness

And that I loved her for not choosing me

The is no fairness in this fight

No sanctuary from our own minds

Each morning bathing in the light

of small victories

Short lived

I am thankful

For my consuming thoughts

The gift of words that come with sacrifice of self

For a heart that beats on against hardened walls

In her broken thrumming I hear a song of survival

Ascendance from my own unbecoming

Ophelia rising

She has a whole history without me

Dark days where she did not expect the sun to rise

Her skin tells me she cried for help

But not one came

I cannot heal her old wounds

I will just make sure the new ones

Never touch her soul

Never slice through her perfection

Her past was not mine

But her future will be

We may never be us again

But promise me

We will never be strangers

When you look for me

You will find me

Right where you left us

I will smile and say

There you are love

I've waited for you

We spend our youth

Trying to feel alive

And our second coming

Dulling the knife's edge

Against raw skin

Afraid to feel again

Now when the sun shines on my face

I turn my seeking eyes upwards

I don't raise my hands to shield my beloved

Or close my eyes against her harshness

I am myself defenseless against the light

I show her my burnt edges

Her flames reach every corner of my doubts

She is the only love I allow to consume me

Engulf my darkness and leave me to ashes

I hope you find peace

And if you do not

I pray there is love

If there is none

I will search for you in the stars

Shining through your suffering

To light my way to you

If you see my mother

Tell her I suffered her fate

But triumphed in her wake

I am getting used to how my new flesh

Sits upon my bones

After tearing myself apart for you

And if we cannot be

Then I will stay in this place

Make my home in the relentless wondering

Nestled in the clutches of what could have been

Just to be devoured by what is

It is not enough

To just survive you

She has starved my demons

Gently dispelled my childish fears

They cower in her presence

My caged inhibitions break away

She waits for me at the door

A small voice closing the space between

You can come out now

A hand slowly reaches for me

Light forming around the face behind it

I instinctively know she has been here

Outstretched and waiting for much too long

For me to recognize her

My last hope

There it is

Just out of reach

My wrists

Were bound

I gnawed lose my heart to be free

This empty cavity still hums

Impersonating life

Soul be still

Thoughts numb

Faint sounds of unbecoming

All that was sacrificed

Remains in the hollows of my chest

She beats on

I pray she makes it

I know we don't all make it

Sunken eyes and weighted tongue

The end was kinder than the beginnings

The light was warm, it led me here

You will breathe again

Your lungs will expand without his heavy hand

The passing hours will swallow your cries

Bite back the urge to succumb to old wounds

Soon, my dear

You will be soft enough to hold

The sharpened edge will dull

Pink hue will tint your cheeks

Where bruised ego once left its stain

Keep your eyes fixed on the sun

I pray she makes it

I see myself in her innocent gaze

Small eyes taking in this strange place from the passenger seat

Time passing quickly out the window

A reflection of me in her youthful stare

Soaking in the immensity of the outside world

Enough to fill those slender arms

I lie and say what a beautiful day

My smile cracks to make conversation

Suspicion growing under her delicate lashes

She sees spring approaching

Eternal summers wait for her

The truth has no season

Sharp edges will take your softness

Cold hearts will take your warmth

You'll lay in empty arms with full lips

For the right words that go unsaid

Left on sidewalks collecting your pride

Scooping them up like pennies for thoughts

Lost to passing time

Instead I peer out her window

In awe

I must believe there is something beyond the glass

For both of us

My right arm begins to shake again

My left hand is aware of your absence

Tell me how brave I was for loving you

Only I know the cost

I will find you

One strong enough to deafen the screams of past

Enclosing me in unbreakable bonds

Even though I am painful to hold

They will stay

At 3am

When I am pacing hallways

Helpless in my own undoing

Hanging on the fringes of sanity

They will know

That even though I beg for an ending

To pull me down from sullen skies

Anchoring my burdens to their own

Like gravity falling back into subdued earth

I will find in you my home

Love was not as I had thought

She was raw fingers grazing the edge of consciousness

The bones of withered intentions

Blossoming

Familiar voices calling you home again

The air filled with the faint scent of decaying youth

Love was not a martyr

She was bare feet and bloodstained knees

Unearthing bond, frail insecurity

Yet in every place we buried her

She grew

I walked from your hold into a steady rain

Obscure footprints leaving proof of my slow decent

Through muddied memories

Our madness reflecting in seething puddles

Inferior efforts to stay adrift are futile

Huddled masses of limbs clinging to bitter endings

Love passes through our grasp like fraying rope

We lose the ones that meant the most

There is no triumph in being the sole survivor

I release you with trembling resonance

We still speak truth submerged in beds of lies

Our condition is self-inflicted

We are beyond saving

Succumbing to her weight in the end

Freeing the heavy burden of flesh

I held the frail figure in my worn grip

Tracing the marks on her body like constellations

Blood saturates her right arm

Where her heart once hung on her sleeve

Remnants of a plucked rib cage

Broken from the inside out

She wore her skin like wrinkled armor

Their names carved into her fragile branches

I placed stones into her hollow chest

Sinking through the murkiness

Limbs intertwined

Her existence was my own tragic decent

There is no safe house for lost innocence

I cannot harbor her naive nature against an attack

Her sunken spirit surfaces in my reflection

I have stopped for answers in her pleading eyes

She sees what I have become without the burden of her

She reaches for me on the outskirts of my sanity

My beautiful sacrifice

Slowly I fell into a deep love

Into the covers of her Sunday slumber

Her heart was in a million pieces

Existing only on the pages of her favorite books

Eyes holding secrets of unkempt madness

A harmonious disposition with flimsy edges

She was finally free from the burden of their conviction

Shoulders rising from the weight of carrying self-loathing

After years of fighting to own her value

At last I love myself

His arms

Held my crumbling disposition in place

I forgot that I hated myself

In those arms

We come to an impasse

We are both defeated

I kiss her head, a peaceful goodbye

The girl I was deserves a proper farewell

I let her bury herself deep in my chest

I will give her the respect she sought in life

The security she longed for was always in me

I save her from herself

I know that in her parting days

She was kissed as she deserved

Accepted apologies that lay buried under their tongues

Forgave gracefully as we each turned her away

The unsought misgivings of saints

A language of feelings that our fingers had gone numb to

It was not intended for us to preserve these delicate

Impressions she left upon our skin

But I know this, when our time had ceased

She had not love, but became it

I spoke unto the night

Like an old companion waiting patiently

I released you to him

Your love no longer held weight on my lungs

Breathing in the dense stars filled with you

I could not confine the immensity of our universe

To one sky

Exhaling the constellations that lead me here

What was once written above us has manifested

Into a scattered destiny

The only light left, a blanket of stardust

I will never fear the darkness

It will always be where I hide you

An infinity of lost intentions

I release you

Bedtime Story

My dear, never be afraid of falling

There is freedom in the ethereal sky

on the other side of your caged defenses

Do not fear the heights, but take heed in your flight

Recall the impression of gravel pressed into your open palms

The pieces we must sacrifice to the soil

Some of our landings must be lessons

Try not to lose faith in your own wings little bird

One day there may be one strong enough to catch you

Brave enough to hold you

And good enough to love you

Until then my dove

Jump

She wasn't the kind of girl that you give flowers

He showed up at her doorstep with bouquets of words

To heal her lonely hours

Yellow daffodils from Wordsworth's tongue

River banks with wild thyme from Shakespeare's summer dreams

He plucked her a magic rose from Thomas himself

Walking in gardens full of forever behind Tennyson

Dwelling in the shadow of Krizzan, chests full of wild lilies

And if that were not enough to fill up her thoughts

A flight on Longfellow's soul like wings

Hushed whispers of Dickenson's hiding spot

The sun came out behind her eyes

And rain slipped down her cheeks

Amongst the weeds and tangled vines

She chose to bloom for me

Morning brings a weighted chest

And heavy step

The faint rhythm under damp skin tells me

I have survived another night

I turn to him, my only refuge

The war inside me fears his light

Raw nerves exposed by subtle touch

Light passes through open wounds

Defensive soul succumbs to peace

Sharp mind & brittle bone

Heavy spirit drudge on

Still seeking solace from the night

She was the best of us

The child, the woman

& you turned your back on girls like her

The ones with past laments chiseled into skin

An illiterate audience

Vacant seats

You left her with no voice

She set herself on fire

To light the way out

Fueled by her own unbecoming

Refusing to be a dull likeness of self

She is the sun

And now you are all forced to look up

There are still things I cannot write

But the weight of those words

Are too heavy for paper and pen

And when you see me again

I will not be a pretty soul

Lost in a sea of strange faces

I will not be the fire

Nor the phoenix

No, what remains will be ash

You burned me at the stake

For your demons, I could not defeat

It may have been my name

On the stone

But I left long before

You wrote my fate

Move forward with grace

Where one steps, another crawls

Fists tight, dry mouth fixed in defiance

Flesh & dirt embedded under finger nails

You will not bury me here

Not in this ground

Not on your terms

I see my own reflection

The girl I could not save

Cowers in my shadow

The victim and the abuser

Share one skin

& on this day I rise

I became a shield

The moment I held you

The glow of motherhood

Only we know

In those first hours

How our minds begin to wage a war with the world

I cannot protect her from

Unworthy hands and empty promise

Behind the gleam of a mother

A reckoning

They leave us with empty wombs

Eyes filled to the brim

Our bodies spilling over

Faltering step and vacancy sign

My flesh, a condemned property

No entry

The sins of our youth will linger

He did not take the best of you

She gently tucks them in at night

A dim light, white flag

There are still those that search the rubble

Finding our pieces adrift

Slowing the waters

Mouths doused in serenity and wine

The sweet taste of redemption

Every touch, coaxing you to live

Save her

There she was

Looking back at me

A girl I will never know

She resides in between

I hope you let her feel the sunshine on her face

From time to time

We were not just meant to pass through

No, look beyond the fog of your contention

These souls were created to intersect

To crash

Our glorious endings

Splayed out on paper

Smudged in truth

This is our purpose

To begin again

She had every right to disappear

I found her

Washed up on abandoned shoreline

Disoriented from misuse

Mangled sentiment, heavy soul

He failed to count his blessings

Her affliction, the price paid for one sided affection

So, I numbered the stars in her eyes

Counted the ten fingers intertwined with mine

Penned the hours to the pace of her steps

Hesitant at first, then sure with time

The girl I found, come back to life

I told the moon about you

He tried to convince me that I still loved the darkness

I knew he saw your light all over me

He released his clutch around my chest,

the tight grip on my wrists

He lost his only glimpse of the sun

Whilst burning in my midst

Give me a day of peace

Of sunlight and ashes

Smudged on my cheek

The sky has been falling

For decades it seems

Cry out, stifled voices

Await your relief

This burden uneasy

Our symphony, a plea

In the lies, we've mistaken

Our truth was not free

Debt owed in ransom

Empty cradles we keep

Wake me in the stillness

Huddled whim

Bent at knees

Oh, empty promise

Of war's end and peace

He called me second chance

Beautiful and strong

How could I become anything else but love

My last chance

Has returned

My lungs fill with the hope of him

The morning brings new hope

The night was long

I thought myself one with the moon

Until you walked in

Dressed in the likeness of dawn

Just promise this

That you will never run out of these words the ones that spill over

Blood & holy water

Let my soul

Drown in you

Washing away all that I thought

Had made me unworthy

Of such love

There was an unhinged madness in her core

Detached smile, bared teeth

Shackled thought and twisted gaze

Steady hand

I reached inside to pull her out

Dry throats

We choke on their ides of deliverance

Hold tight to crumbling walls

Let all that touched her

Collapse at our feet

The liberated child

Cage unlatched

She stays

Isolation keeps us captive

Subdues the untamed thoughts

Claims our humanity

Stay put sweet child

where the world cannot shake your delicate frame into submission

One by one

All of my abusers

Became dust

&

I walked into the light

There was no rebirth

Or awakening

Just a sunset

New love

The smell of wet pavement

And the sound of redemption beneath my feet

The truth is

She never came up for air

There was no struggle against the current

And I could have sworn

I saw her smile

Through unrelenting waves

Silently we succumb to our fate

I imagine she has found herself on some deserted shoreline

Where time stops beneath bare feet

From under swaying palm tree

I see her smile

I don't talk to the moon

She comes to me in darkness

She's healing quickly and I envy the fight

Unyielding spirit

Among the sky

Solitary in her plight

I don't speak of the sun

My sweet sacrifice to the gods

She is the light that burns from the inside

I know her pain, the flame I cannot quell within her

But without the fire, the phoenix within us could not rise

She is the reason we look above

The reason I have survived this long

The stars are ever changing in my palms

They curl into me like an infant

My arms are full

Until empty

The sky is vast

She has no ruler

No consequence

Just an endless dance

against time

I looked like Jackie O

She was born in New York

Like you

You would have known that

or like Audrey

You always said I was an Audrey

I held the smallest version I had of you

Close to my black lace dress

Tiny cowgirl boots dangling past my hem

Sunflowers in her hair, your favorite

He promised me better, your son

The day you left us

I wanted to believe

I was his June

But I was Jackie

I wasn't as strong

Or

Brave

Or as good as you

But

You were my mother too

I saw you

You were a glass house

A tropical flower

In a desert

A misplaced white cross

on the side of the road

I know you found your way

Beyond the prisms of this confined space

Resting eternally in tranquil warm waters

I still see you

In her

All that held you to the earth

Your strength

Your gracious soul

Safely kept

Your daughter's spirit

The world is opening

I found comfort in closing myself to it

I owed no excuses to the outside

The doorway held no expectation of me

I curled up inside corners of self

I had long ignored

I nurtured the introvert

Gifted myself idleness

Besotted with the lilting hymnals of crickets

The still evening air of Summer

Dewy morning with no assurance

Life without promise

I will return to myself

When Autumn answers

IV –
TRANSCENDENCE

Dancing on a razors edge

Defiance in my blood

Even when I take up the sun with my curves

I feel unworthy of her likeness

We are taught the shadows best suit our rebellion to shrink

With our swelling ambitions pouring over an underwire bra

Your eyes would still linger on the lack of space between my thighs

I curled my body into corners

Wrapped my legs around men's egos

Choking down my intellect for your comfort

You leave no room for sprawling limbs to grow here

Yet in our womb you demand that my walls expand

to make a home

My flesh is my land, one you can never claim as you own

It is not a green pasture for unattended men

To pillage and diminish

You will not raise your flag over my head

And hold me to a standard you could not lie beneath

You have paid in full for your plight to dominate

There are no good girls here, only angry women

With the history of their ancestors burning in their bellies

With an unfinished fight raging in their daughters

Don't interrupt – we are speaking now

Life wasn't beautiful before this

It was mascara running down the faces of girls

Stumbling out of dark alley ways

Me too echoing in deaf courtrooms

Black lives beaten into black asphalt

An all lives banter dribbling off of the lips of our elders

Our leaders holding the walls of hatred together

with shaking morals

Yet we came out in masses

Shouldering the burden of change

Setting fire to our cities to bring light to injustice

A new voice, a generation rising from under us

We lift them high enough to reach the tops of mountains

we may never see

But it's there in the eyes of suckling babes

Hope delivered from the ashes of a burning nation

A new declaration

For the good of all must triumph

And the oppressor must cease his hold on the neck of this country

I will be your shield

I will be the barricade

My body will cover yours

Because you are worth this

My last breath

You are worth the fight

Your history was marred

Equality never touched the shores

They left you on

I will stand with you

Until our weary legs shake the system

Until the cries for equality are heard

Until their statues bleed

The tears of injustice

Until our children continue the battle

After us

We will show them

A way without violence

A future with freedom for all

They were my Bronte Sisters

Salt water cheeks

Pressed against my chest

All of my yesterdays

My sweet sacrifice

Set off into the world

Fiery tongue and sharpened mind

Swaddled rebellion

Armored in generational truth

I dressed them in pink

The likeness of a blushing sunset

Burning into deep red

We all looked up

Red, white, blue

Turned to black

The injustice

Fresh on our cheeks

Flickering neon signs

Illuminating

The sins of a nation

On bloodied asphalt

They tried to clean the stain of inhumanity

But their names rise to the surface

Calling us to stand with them

I sat next to him in group therapy

He had a scar under his right eye

Our legs twitched in unison

His left hand had a tremor

My demons lurked in the corners, my shame

His made deafening booms

And marched on inside of his chest

Boots beating upon his heart

The thrumming voices of every brother

He could not save

There was no emotion

Blank stare into unreachable recovery

When it was my turn

He stood behind my chair weeping

I was struggling to keep upright

As I sank deeper into recollection

He hoovered

Guarding over my subconscious

There are wars inside us now

For a moment we shoulder the battle together

To catch our breath

To understand

The aftermath of haunted souls

There are many who suffer

And few who stand for the fallen

There are no victims here

Only warriors on their knees

I was born on both sides of the fence

Teetering on a razors edge

My mere existence was in defiance

My father's last battle cry

Or

My mother's last goodbye

Was I abandoned or was she

But who remembers the lost daughters

Born from teenage angst

and suppressed convictions

Pink blanketed truth

Wrapped in misconception

Fist tight

On the stolen silver spoon

When does the child

Become liberated

From generational

Afflictions

I am every brown girl

Mossy soul

Toes dusted in earth

Deep rooted sorrows

Feet stamped onto a small patch of green

You continue to sweep from under me

Half-blood heart

The desert and the sea cry out within

Two worlds diverge

The war inside

Spirit tells me

This fight

Is mine

Take head earth's daughter

You are not homeless

Wandering is not a crime

You were digested by a savage system

That took away all of your human boundaries

And carved their own rules on your skin with dirty nails

Nails that sealed the coffin of your fate

long before you had the chance to fight

Victims with no voice

Deemed unfit for this world

And yet we burn human decency to fan the flames of false hope

And we carry the weight of our struggle

On each other's backs

And never our own

This is a strange land

We have found our footing on

It lacks solidity

The firmness of our

Convictions

Lay heavily

On our need to feel superior

Empathy was a weakness

And those who felt everything

At once

Held society together

On their broken bones

Just to hear the screams

above

Freedom is coming

But not for us

On this Eve

Of idle promise

Come to us softy

We scare so easily now

Dance with us

Around our empty living rooms

Rejoice in the life

After dying

The deafening silence

Of all we have survived

Masked poetics

Muffled politics

These frozen years

Have made this place cold

The hands of time

Endure

Brushing against death

The clock has failed us

Again

I lost my faith in your god

Tucked in a basket

In a vacant tomb

I watched

Good people

Do nothing

And I could not sit beside them

Any longer

On an empty pew

On a Sunday

I lost all hope

In a book

The business of

Sacred words you

Sold for entry into

The gates

Is there a god

Somewhere

Losing faith in us

In his creation

That looks nothing like

Him

That looks nothing

Like me

I wrote about you

Before I held you

You were an inclination

A child's longing

A sister

A small mirrored version

Of self

I felt you coursing through me

Before you reached your mother's strong arms

She felt it too

Giving birth to expanding cells

That host the cosmos

Under the one sky

The universe stopped

In reverence

There is another

Born with the fire

Touched soul

The remnants of earth under her nails

Toes dipped in the soiled ruins

Of lost daughters

Eva, the beginning and the end

Guide us

Home

MORE ABOUT THE BOOK

Ophelia Rising is laced with the passionate beauty, fullness and longing of Elizabeth Barrett Browning, rounded by the intense rebellion of Emily Dickinson's feminist spirit. This is an epic rant, a sacred rage of love greater than its bloody parts. This Ophelia speaks directly to the broken deities of lost and abandoned girls, shedding her skin, rising as survivor, intact and whole, a divine warrior unafraid to love and be loved without apology. To heal and be healed. To take her place in the world as open protest, fully alive as the woman she was born to be.

— S.A. Griffin, author of *Pandemic Soul Music*

"Ophelia Rising" is an epic poem encompassing loss, survival, tragedy and triumph, not only for the writer, but for all of us. As the words spoke to me, I began to hear echoes of John Coltrane's masterpiece, "A Love Supreme," a suite in four parts: Acknowledgement, Resolution, Pursuance, and Psalm. Like Coltrane, O.R. presents four sections: Ophelia's Last Words, Unbecoming, Rising, Transcendence. And, like Coltrane, she pursues a spiritual quest culminating in those last words: *Guide us...Home.*

This work is a project surrounded by love. And, on a final note, do NOT skip over the forward.

— Puma Perl, poet/writer, Birthdays Before and After (Beyond Baroque Press)

The poems in O.R.'s *Ophelia Rising* are vivid and seductive, sharp and sweet like licking honey from a razor blade. A superb debut collection!

— Richard Modiano, Director Emeritus Beyond Baroque Literary/Arts Center. Author of *The Forbidden Lunchbox.*

O.R.'s poems explore themes of family, abandonment, and romantic heartbreak to reveal love's strength, fragility, and complexities in its many forms. And while O.R. shows us that love is not perfect—it can be bruised and bountiful, saintly and sin-bitten—it has the power to exist within the most beautiful lines our lives have written.

– Rich Ferguson, L.A. poet/spoken-word performer

ABOUT THE AUTHOR

O.R. was born with words overflowing from her lineage. She is a mother first to three adult daughters and a wife to second chance. O.R. has been writing poetry since she was a child and studied English Literature in college. She was a high school English teacher for a short time and has stayed in the field of education. California has been her birthplace and where she resides currently with one foot in the mountains and the other in the ocean. O.R spends her days with children and her evenings on the track playing roller derby with her local league. It has been an outlet for the writer for over a decade.

MORE BOOKS ON PUNK HOSTAGE PRESS

Danny Baker
Fractured -- 2012

A Razor
Better Than a Gun in A Knife Fight - 2012
Drawn Blood: Collected Works
From D.B.P.LTD., 1985-1995 - 2012
Beaten Up Beaten Down – 2012
Small Catastrophes in A Big World - 2012
Half- Century Status – 2013
Days of Xmas Poems - 2014
Puro Purismo - 2021

Iris Berry
The Daughters of Bastards – 2012
All That Shines Under the Hollywood Sign – 2019
The Trouble with Palm Trees - 2021
Gas Station Etiquette - 2022

C.V. Auchterlonie
Impress - 2012

Yvonne De la Vega
Tomorrow, Yvonne - Poetry & Prose for Suicidal Egoists - 2012

Carolyn Srygley- Moore
Miracles Of the Blog: A Series - 2012

Rich Ferguson
8th & Agony -2012

Jack Grisham
Untamed -2013
Code Blue: A Love Story ~ Limited Edition—2014
Pulse of the World. Arthur Chance, Punk Rock Detective - 2022

Dennis Cruz
Moth Wing Tea - 2013
The Beast Is We - 2018

Frank Reardon
Blood Music - 2013

Pleasant Gehman
Showgirl Confidential—2013
Rock 'N' Roll Witch: A Memoir of Sex Magick, Drugs, And Rock 'N' Roll - 2022

Hollie Hardy
How To Take a Bullet and Other Survival Poems—2014

SB Stokes
History Of Broken Love Things—2014

MORE BOOKS ON PUNK HOSTAGE PRESS

Joel Landmine
Yeah, Well...—2014
Things Change - 2022
Michele McDannold
Stealing The Midnight from A Handful of Days—2014
A.D. Winans
Dead Lions—2014
S.A. Griffin
Dreams Gone Mad with Hope - 2014
Nadia Bruce- Rawlings
Scars - 2014
Driving in The Rain - 2020
Lee Quarnstrom
WHEN I WAS A DYNAMITER, Or, how a Nice Catholic Boy Became a Merry Prankster, a Pornographer, and a Bridegroom Seven Times - 2014
Alexandra Naughton
I Will Always Be Your Whore/Love Songs for Billy Corgan- 2014
You Could Never Objectify Me More Than I've Already Objectified Myself -2015
Maisha Z Johnson
No Parachutes to Carry Me Home - 2015
Michael Marcus
#1 Son and Other Stories - 2017
Danny Garcia
LOOKING FOR JOHNNY, The Legend of Johnny Thunders - 2018
William S. Hayes
Burden of Concrete - 2020
Todd Moore
Dillinger's Thompson - 2020
Dan Denton
$100-A-Week Motel – 2021
Jack Henry
Driving W/ Crazy, living with madness—2021
Joe Donnelly
So Cal: Dispatches from the End of The World—2022
Patrick O'Neil
Anarchy at The Circle K – On the Road with Dead Kennedys, TSOL, Flipper, Subhumans and… Heroin – 2022
Richard Modiano
The Forbidden Lunchbox – 2023
S.A. Griffin
Pandemic Soul Music - 2023
Shawna Kenney
I Was A Teenage Dominatrix - 2023